NAME THAT MAMMAL!

By Santana Hunt

Gareth Stevens
PUBLISHING

Please visit our website, www.garethstevens.com. For a free color catalog of all our high-quality books, call toll free 1-800-542-2595 or fax 1-877-542-2596.

Cataloging-in-Publication Data

Names: Hunt, Santana.
Title: Name that mammal! / Santana Hunt.
Description: New York : Gareth Stevens Publishing, 2017. | Series: Guess that animal! | Includes index.
Identifiers: ISBN 9781482447569 (pbk.) | ISBN 9781482447460 (library bound) | ISBN 9781482447057 (6 pack)
Subjects: LCSH: Mammals–Juvenile literature.
Classification: LCC QL706.2 H86 2017 | DDC 599–dc23

Published in 2017 by
Gareth Stevens Publishing
111 East 14th Street, Suite 349
New York, NY 10003

Designer: Andrea Davison-Bartolotta
Editor: Kristen Nelson

Photo credits: Cover, p. 1 Eric Isselee/Shutterstock.com; p. 5 Mr. Suttipon Yakham/Shutterstock.com; pp. 7, 9 Vera Zinkova/Shutterstock.com; pp. 11, 13 jadimages/Shutterstock.com; pp. 15, 17 Ger Bosma Photos/Shutterstock.com; pp. 19, 21 enciktat/Shutterstock.com.

Printed in the United States of America

CPSIA compliance information: Batch #CS16GS: For further information contact Gareth Stevens, New York, New York at 1-800-542-2595.

CONTENTS

Boldface words appear in the glossary.

What's a Mammal?

Mammals are animals that breathe air, have a backbone, and have fur or hair. They have live young that often drink milk from their mother's body. Dogs, cats, and people are all mammals! Can you guess the ones in this book?

What's on the Cover?

It's a hedgehog! Hedgehogs are covered with sharp **spines**. When they feel **threatened**, they curl into a spiny ball no predator would want to eat!

Hair and Hoofs

Like many mammals, this one moves around on four legs! It can be many colors, from white to black to pretty reddish browns. It has a long mane and tail. Its teeth are flat in order to better chew the plants it likes to eat. Do you know this mammal?

It's a horse! Horses don't have toes like people do. They have hoofs, which are hard, curved coverings on their feet. Horses are fast, too!

Mud Lover

This mammal rolls in the mud to cool down! It's found on farms and in the wild all over the world. It's often known for being pink, but it can be black, brown, or a mix, too. What's the mammal?

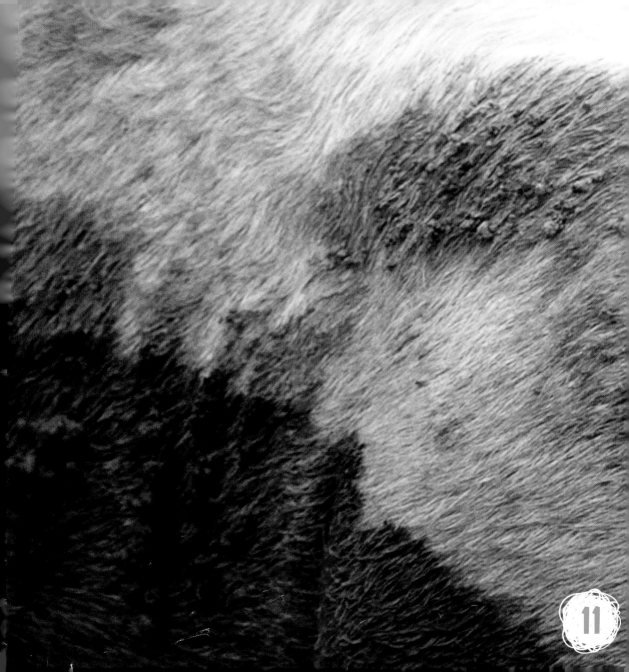

It's a pig! Baby pigs, or piglets, drink their mother's milk for 3 to 5 weeks. In that time, they more than double how much they weighed at birth! Adult pigs can be between 300 and 700 pounds (136 and 318 kg).

Hop to It!

Have you ever seen a tail like this one? It belongs to a mammal that's known for its long back feet and strong back legs. It moves around by hopping! What mammal could it be?

It's a rabbit! Cottontail rabbits, like this one, are named for their small, fuzzy tails that look like cotton balls. Like other rabbits, cottontails are **herbivores**. They eat grasses and lettuces when they can and sticks and bark during winter.

Large Cat

Since all cats are mammals, the largest cat in the world is one, too! This mammal is easy to **identify** because of its orange fur, white belly, and black or brown stripes. Can you guess which big cat this is?

It's a tiger! Tigers are **carnivores**. They use their long, sharp teeth when catching food. Some kinds of tigers have already died out. Other kinds are **endangered**, but you can see this amazing mammal in zoos all over the world.

GLOSSARY

carnivore: an animal that eats meat

endangered: in danger of dying out

herbivore: an animal that only eats plants

identify: to find out the name of something

spine: one of the sharp, stiff hairs growing from a mammal

threaten: to give signs that harm is likely coming

FOR MORE INFORMATION

BOOKS

Beaumont, Holly. *Why Do Monkeys and Other Mammals Have Fur?* Chicago, IL: Heinemann Raintree, 2016.

Boothroyd, Jennifer. *Endangered and Extinct Mammals.* Minneapolis, MN: Lerner Publications Company, 2014.

Coupe, Robert. *Cats of the Wild.* New York, NY: PowerKids Press, 2015.

WEBSITES

Mammals
kids.nationalgeographic.com/animals/hubs/mammals/
Learn more about mammals and other kinds of animals.

What Makes a Mammal?
kids.sandiegozoo.org/animals/mammals
See many pictures and read more about what features mammals share.

23

INDEX